Teaching Prosocial Behavior to Antisocial Youth

Workshop Supplement

A Workshop
with
Arnold P. Goldstein, Ph.D.

Research Press
2612 North Mattis Avenue
Champaign, Illinois 61822
www.researchpress.com

Contents

Part 3
The Skillstreaming Setting: Creating Safe Schools

Part 4

Skillstreaming: Reducing Resistance, Increasing Motivation, and Enhancing Generalization

Introduction

This *Workshop Supplement* contains copies of the essential overheads used by Dr. Arnold P. Goldstein in his videotaped workshop presentation, *Teaching Prosocial Behavior to Antisocial Youth*. This video program is presented in six parts:

Part 1

Skillstreaming: History and Development   52:00

Part 2

Skillstreaming: Curriculum and Training Procedures   45:00

Part 3

The Skillstreaming Setting: Creating Safe Schools   54:00

Part 4

Skillstreaming: Reducing Resistance, Increasing Motivation, and Enhancing Generalization   56:00

Part 5

Aggression Replacement Training   50:00

Part 6

The Prepare Curriculum
and
Antisocial Youth:
Productive and Unproductive Intervention Strategies   51:00

This *Workshop Supplement* will serve as a useful guide as you view Dr. Goldstein's workshop. Each page is keyed to the corresponding overhead in the video program and summarizes the main points and content presented by Dr. Goldstein.

Dr. Goldstein's presentation focuses on three research-based interventions for working with aggressive adolescents and children—Skillstreaming, Aggression Replacement Training, and the Prepare Curriculum. He presents the rationale and background underlying these companion interventions and discusses the details and dynamics of how to implement them in schools and other settings.

Another focus of the workshop is the all-important issue of violence and aggression in schools. Dr. Goldstein presents "best practice" solutions for creating safe schools in which prosocial intervention programs can be facilitated. He emphasizes the importance of enhancing generalization so that prosocial skills learned in the training setting will actually transfer to other settings and endure over time. Dr. Goldstein concludes his workshop with a discussion of productive and unproductive intervention strategies for aggressive youth.

Dr. Goldstein has a career-long interest, as both researcher and practitioner, in difficult-to-reach clients. Since 1980, his main research and psychoeducational focus has been youth violence. He is the Director of the Syracuse University Center for Research on Aggression, which he founded in 1981.

His research, curriculum development, and teaching have centered on helping aggressive adolescents and children replace antisocial, aggressive behaviors with constructive, alternative means of seeking life satisfaction and effectiveness. Dr. Goldstein is the author of numerous scholarly publications as well as research-based curricula for working with troubled and troubling youth. The curricula are discussed in Dr. Goldstein's videotaped workshop presentation and referenced throughout this *Workshop Supplement*.

Currently professor emeritus of education and psychology at Syracuse University, Dr. Goldstein joined the university's Psychology Department in 1963 and both taught there and directed its Psychotherapy Center. In 1985 he joined the university's Division of Special Education and in 1990 helped organize and codirect the New York State Task Force on Juvenile Gangs. Dr. Goldstein is a member of the American Psychological Association Commission on Youth Violence; a member of the Council of Representatives, International Society for Research on Aggression; and associate editor of the journal *Aggressive Behavior*.

He has received many awards for his outstanding work in psychology and education, among them the Award of Excellence (1990) from the Juvenile Justice Trainer's Association; the Blackburn Award for Significant Contributions (1991) from the National Association of Juvenile Correctional Agencies; the U.S. Office of Juvenile Justice and Delinquency Prevention's Model Program Award (1994) for The Prosocial Gang Project; the American Psychological Association's Committee on Children, Youth, and Families Outstanding Career Contribution Award (1996); and the Senior Scientist Award (1996) from the School Psychology Division of the American Psychological Association.

Dr. Goldstein can be contacted at the Center for Research on Aggression, Syracuse University, 805 South Crouse Avenue, Syracuse, New York 13244. Phone: (315) 443-9641.

Part 1
Skillstreaming:
History and Development

Dr. Goldstein introduces his workshop by discussing the impact that aggressive youth can have on the teachers and staff who work with them. He continues with a discussion of the development of childhood aggression, focusing on the sources that contribute to its development, such as coercive parenting and peer rejection.

Dr. Goldstein then discusses the basis of the Skillstreaming approach in social learning theory and the psychological skills training perspective, which involves active and deliberate teaching of desirable behaviors to skill-deficient youth. He emphasizes the particular value of this approach in working with youth from lower socioeconomic backgrounds. He concludes his presentation with a discussion of the Skillstreaming procedures of modeling, role-playing, performance feedback, and generalization training.

The Skillstreaming approach and training procedures are discussed in detail in the following publications:

Goldstein, A. P., & McGinnis, E. (1997). *Skillstreaming the adolescent: New strategies and perspectives for teaching prosocial skills* (rev. ed.). Champaign IL: Research Press.

McGinnis, E., & Goldstein, A. P. (1997). *Skillstreaming the elementary school child: New strategies and perspectives for teaching prosocial skills* (rev. ed.). Champaign IL: Research Press.

McGinnis, E., & Goldstein, A. P. (1990). *Skillstreaming in early childhood: Teaching prosocial skills to the preschool and kindergarten child.* Champaign IL: Research Press.

Goldstein, A. P., & McGinnis, E. (1988). *The Skillstreaming video: How to teach students prosocial skills* [Videotape]. Champaign IL: Research Press.

Sources of Burnout

- **Inadequate orientation**
- **Work overload**
- **Lack of stimulation**
- **Inadequate leadership and supervision**
- **Social isolation**
- **Role conflict and ambiguity**
- **Nonparticipation in decision-making**
- **Poor parent-teacher relations**
- **Student disruptiveness**
- **Student violence**
- **Student apathy**

Teacher Burnout

Emotional Exhaustion

Stress dimension of burnout

Feel overextended, depleted, frustrated, minimalist approach to teaching

Depersonalization

Interpersonal dimension of burnout

Detached from co-workers, punitive toward students, callous, negative, low expectation of student success

Reduced Personal Accomplishment

Self-evaluative dimension of burnout

Feel less competent and less productive at work

From "The Client Role in Staff Burnout," by C. Maslach, 1978, *Journal of Special Issues, 34,* pp. 111-124.

Physical Abuse

Punch

Kick

Shake

Choke

Burn

Shoot

Stab

Smack

Spank

Swat

Verbal Abuse

1. ## Character Attacks

2. ## Competence Attacks
   Example: "How could you be so stupid?"

3. ## Background Attacks
   Example: "You're just like your father, a loser."

4. ## Physical Appearance Attacks
   Example: "Must you always look like a slob?"

5. ## Maledictions
   Example: "You'll never amount to anything."

6. ## Teasing

7. ## Ridicule

8. ## Threats

9. ## Swearing

10. ## Nonverbal Emblems
    Example: Making derogatory faces

From "Teaching Students to Understand and Control Verbal Aggression," by D. A. Infante, 1995, *Communication Education, 44,* pp. 51-63.

Aggression as Addiction

- **A long-term stable behavior, repetitively enacted**

- **Subjective compulsion to use it**

- **Reduced ability to control or reduce it, in frequency or intensity**

- **Frequent relapses**
    Negative emotional states
    Interpersonal conflicts
    Situations where used before

- **Initiated and sustained by both person and environment**

- **Yields short-term pleasure despite long-term negatives**

- **Used in response to, and to relieve, stress, negative mood, general arousal**

- **Often encouraged and rewarded by (peer, family) "enablers"**

- **Often experienced with a "rush" of pleasure/ excitement**

- **Frequently accompanied by denial (e.g., attribution of blame)**

- **Preoccupied with others' use of the behavior (e.g., aggressive TV viewing)**

- **High rate of health risk, injury, death**

- **Taught, encouraged, rewarded by larger society**

Coercive Parenting

- **Frequent, vague commands**
- **Low levels of warmth, involvement, empathy**
- **Strict and lax monitoring of child's behavior**
- **Nattering**
  Empty threats
  Pleading
  Nagging
  Scolding
- **Threatening, yelling, corporal punishment**
  High frequency
  Noncontingent
- **Start-ups, counterattacks, escalation of conflicts**
- **Inconsistent reaction after escalation**
  Giving in
  Exploding
- **Negative reinforcement of child's coerciveness**

From *Antisocial Boys*, by G. R. Patterson, J. B. Reid, & T. J. Dishion, 1992, Eugene OR: Castalia Press.

Development of Aggression in Childhood

Coercive Parenting

↓

Early Aggression

↓

Peer Rejection

↙ ↘

Social Isolation   Attribution of
                          Hostile Intent

↘ ↙

Affiliation with Antisocial Peer Group

↓

Inadequate Social Skills Development

↓

Continued High Levels of Aggressive Behavior

From *Antisocial Boys*, by G. R. Patterson, J. B. Reid, & T. J. Dishion, 1992, Eugene OR: Castalia Press.

Social Class and Psychotherapy

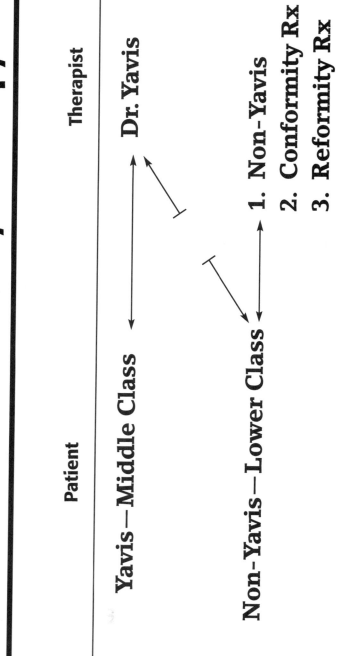

Patient

Therapist

Yavis—Middle Class   Dr. Yavis

Non-Yavis—Lower Class
1. Non-Yavis
2. Conformity Rx
3. Reformity Rx

Social Class and Learning Style

Learning Style		Skillstreaming
Middle class	Lower class	
Motivation	Consequences	Modeling
Empathy	Action	Role-playing
Self-control	External authority	Performance feedback
		Transfer training

Skillstreaming Procedures

Modeling
(Skill Demonstration by Trainers)

+

Role-Playing
(Skill Rehearsal by Youth)

+

Performance Feedback
(By Trainers and All Youth in Group)

+

Generalization Training
(To Increase Both Transfer and Maintenance)

Part 1
Notes

Part 2
Skillstreaming:
Curriculum and Training Procedures

Dr. Goldstein discusses the structure of the Skillstreaming curriculum and its associated training procedures. Beginning with an overview of the 50 skills in the curriculum for adolescents, Dr. Goldstein then discusses the elementary and preschool curricula. He provides samples of student handouts and assessment forms, such as Homework Reports and Parent, Staff, and Student Skillstreaming Checklists, to illustrate the concrete ways in which Skillstreaming is implemented.

Dr. Goldstein describes and demonstrates the purpose and importance of each of the Skillstreaming training steps from the first step of defining the skill through establishing the youth's need for the skill and setting up and conducting the role play to assigning skill homework. He concludes this video with a discussion of the Skillstreaming teaching arrangements, covering such topics as trainer-trainee cultural compatibility, criteria for inclusion/exclusion, placement in the school curriculum, and assessment of program effectiveness.

The Skillstreaming approach and training procedures are discussed in detail in the following publications:

Goldstein, A. P., & McGinnis, E. (1997). *Skillstreaming the adolescent: New strategies and perspectives for teaching prosocial skills* (rev. ed.). Champaign IL: Research Press.

McGinnis, E., & Goldstein, A. P. (1997). *Skillstreaming the elementary school child: New strategies and perspectives for teaching prosocial skills* (rev. ed.). Champaign IL: Research Press.

McGinnis, E., & Goldstein, A. P. (1990). *Skillstreaming in early childhood: Teaching prosocial skills to the preschool and kindergarten child.* Champaign IL: Research Press.

Goldstein, A. P., & McGinnis, E. (1988). *The Skillstreaming video: How to teach students prosocial skills* [Videotape]. Champaign IL: Research Press.

Group I: Beginning Social Skills

1. **Listening**

2. **Starting a Conversation**

3. **Having a Conversation**

4. **Asking a Question**

5. **Saying Thank You**

6. **Introducing Yourself**

7. **Introducing Other People**

8. **Giving a Compliment**

From *Skillstreaming the Adolescent: New Strategies and Perspectives for Teaching Prosocial Skills* (Rev. Ed.), by A. P. Goldstein & E. McGinnis, 1997, Champaign IL: Research Press.

Skillstreaming the Adolescent
Group II: Advanced Social Skills

9. **Asking for Help**

10. **Joining In**

11. **Giving Instructions**

12. **Following Instructions**

13. **Apologizing**

14. **Convincing Others**

From *Skillstreaming the Adolescent: New Strategies and Perspectives for Teaching Prosocial Skills* (Rev. Ed.), by A. P. Goldstein & E. McGinnis, 1997, Champaign IL: Research Press.

Group III: Skills for Dealing with Feelings

15. **Knowing Your Feelings**

16. **Expressing Your Feelings**

17. **Understanding the Feelings of Others**

18. **Dealing with Someone Else's Anger**

19. **Expressing Affection**

20. **Dealing with Fear**

21. **Rewarding Yourself**

From *Skillstreaming the Adolescent: New Strategies and Perspectives for Teaching Prosocial Skills* (Rev. Ed.), by A. P. Goldstein & E. McGinnis, 1997, Champaign IL: Research Press.

Skillstreaming the Adolescent
Group IV: Skill Alternatives to Aggression

22. **Asking Permission**

23. **Sharing Something**

24. **Helping Others**

25. **Negotiation**

26. **Using Self-Control**

27. **Standing Up for Your Rights**

28. **Responding to Teasing**

29. **Avoiding Trouble with Others**

30. **Keeping Out of Fights**

From *Skillstreaming the Adolescent: New Strategies and Perspectives for Teaching Prosocial Skills* (Rev. Ed.), by A. P. Goldstein & E. McGinnis, 1997, Champaign IL: Research Press.

Group V: Skills for Dealing with Stress

31. **Making a Complaint**

32. **Answering a Complaint**

33. **Being a Good Sport**

34. **Dealing with Embarrassment**

35. **Dealing with Being Left Out**

36. **Standing Up for a Friend**

37. **Responding to Persuasion**

38. **Responding to Failure**

39. **Dealing with Contradictory Messages**

40. **Dealing with an Accusation**

41. **Getting Ready for a Difficult Conversation**

42. **Dealing with Group Pressure**

From *Skillstreaming the Adolescent: New Strategies and Perspectives for Teaching Prosocial Skills* (Rev. Ed.), by A. P. Goldstein & E. McGinnis, 1997, Champaign IL: Research Press.

43. **Deciding on Something to Do**

44. **Deciding What Caused a Problem**

45. **Setting a Goal**

46. **Deciding on Your Abilities**

47. **Gathering Information**

48. **Arranging Problems by Importance**

49. **Making a Decision**

50. **Concentrating on a Task**

From *Skillstreaming the Adolescent: New Strategies and Perspectives for Teaching Prosocial Skills* (Rev. Ed.), by A. P. Goldstein & E. McGinnis, 1997, Champaign IL: Research Press.

Skill 2: Starting a Conversation

Steps

1. **Greet the other person.**

2. **Make small talk.**

3. **Decide if the other person is listening.**

4. **Bring up the main topic.**

From *Skillstreaming the Adolescent: New Strategies and Perspectives for Teaching Prosocial Skills* (Rev. Ed.), by A. P. Goldstein & E. McGinnis, 1997, Champaign IL: Research Press.

Skill 25: Negotiating

Steps

1. Decide if you and the other person are having a difference of opinion.

2. Tell the other person what you think about the problem.

3. Ask the other person what he/she thinks about the problem.

4. Listen openly to his/her answer.

5. Think about why the other person might feel this way.

6. Suggest a compromise.

From *Skillstreaming the Adolescent: New Strategies and Perspectives for Teaching Prosocial Skills* (Rev. Ed.), by A. P. Goldstein & E. McGinnis, 1997, Champaign IL: Research Press.

Skill 42: Dealing with Group Pressure

Steps

1. **Think about what the group wants you to do and why.**

2. **Decide what you want to do.**

3. **Decide how to tell the group what you want to do.**

4. **Tell the group what you have decided.**

From *Skillstreaming the Adolescent: New Strategies and Perspectives for Teaching Prosocial Skills* (Rev. Ed.), by A. P. Goldstein & E. McGinnis, 1997, Champaign IL: Research Press.

Skillstreaming in Early Childhood
Skill 7: Asking a Favor
Skill 8: Ignoring

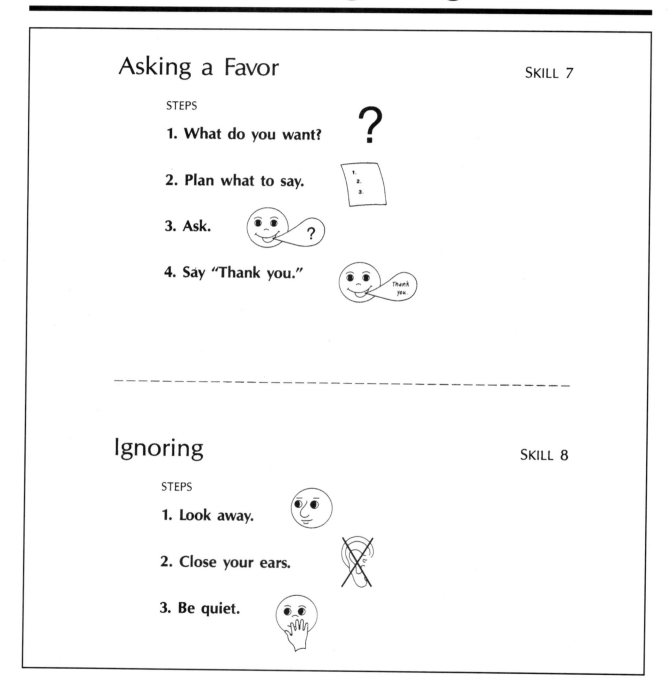

Asking a Favor

SKILL 7

STEPS

1. What do you want?

2. Plan what to say.

3. Ask.

4. Say "Thank you."

Ignoring

SKILL 8

STEPS

1. Look away.

2. Close your ears.

3. Be quiet.

From *Skillstreaming in Early Childhood: Teaching Prosocial Skills to the Preschool and Kindergarten Child–Program Forms*, by E. McGinnis & A. P. Goldstein, 1990, Champaign IL: Research Press.

Skill 10: Ignoring Distractions

STEPS	NOTES FOR DISCUSSION
1. Count to five.	Discuss that counting to five will give the student the time to calm down if frustrated and to recall the rest of the skill steps.
2. Say to yourself, "I won't look. I'll keep on working."	Statements should be spoken aloud during modeling and role-playing.
3. Continue to work.	
4. Say to yourself, "Good for me. I did it!"	Discuss ways of rewarding yourself.

SUGGESTED SITUATIONS

School: Another teacher comes into the room to talk with your teacher.

Home: Your brother or sister tries to distract you from your chores or homework.

Peer group: A classmate tries to get your attention in class or to distract you from a game at recess.

COMMENTS

Each time students ignore a distraction, they may make a check mark on an index card or color a space on one of the Self-Recording Forms from the Program Forms book (see the example in Figure 6, p. 75). Self-recording efforts can then be reinforced if needed.

Rewarding Yourself (Skill 35) is a part of this skill (Step 4). Self-reinforcement may be necessary until the skill can be reinforced by teachers or parents.

From *Skillstreaming the Elementary School Child: New Strategies and Perspectives for Teaching Prosocial Skills* (Rev. Ed.), by E. McGinnis & A. P. Goldstein, 1997, Champaign IL: Research Press.

Skillstreaming Training Steps

1. Define the skill.

2. Model the skill.

3. Establish trainee skill need.

4. Select role-player (main actor).

5. Set up the role-play (co-actor, set the "stage").

6. Conduct the role-play.

7. Provide feedback (order: co-actor, observing trainees, trainers, main actor).

8. Assign skill homework.

9. Select next role-player.

Skill 19: Expressing Affection

Steps

1. **Decide if you have good feelings about the other person.**

2. **Decide if the other person would like to know about your feelings.**

3. **Choose the best way to express your feelings.**

4. **Choose the best time and place to express your feelings.**

5. **Express your feelings in a friendly way.**

From *Skillstreaming the Adolescent: New Strategies and Perspectives for Teaching Prosocial Skills* (Rev. Ed.), by A. P. Goldstein & E. McGinnis, 1997, Champaign IL: Research Press.

Skillstreaming the Adolescent
Homework Report 1

Name: _Josh_   Date: _September 15_

FILL IN DURING THIS CLASS

1. What skill will you use?   _Dealing with Group Pressure_

2. What are the steps for the skill?

    1. Think about what the group wants you to do and why.

    2. Decide what you want to do.

    3. Decide how to tell the group what you want to do.

    4. Tell the group what you have decided.

3. Where will you try the skill?   _At my locker._

4. With whom will you try the skill?   _My friends._

5. When will you try the skill?   _After school._

FILL IN AFTER DOING YOUR HOMEWORK

1. What happened when you did the homework?

    My friends acted like they sort of understood.

2. Which skill steps did you really follow?

    1, 2, and 4.

3. How good a job did you do in using the skill? *(check one)*
   ☐ excellent   ☑ good   ☐ fair   ☐ poor

4. What do you think should be your next homework assignment?

    Try the skill again with the same friends.

From *Skillstreaming the Adolescent–Student Manual*, by A. P. Goldstein & E. McGinnis, 1997, Champaign IL: Research Press.

Skillstreaming the Elementary School Child
Homework Report 1

Name: __Sam_____ Date: ___October 15_____

SKILL: __Responding to Teasing_____

STEPS:

    1. Stop and count to five.

    2. Think about your choices:

        a. Ignore the teasing.

        b. Say how you feel.

        c. Give a reason for the person to stop.

    3. Act out your best choice.

With whom will I try this? _____The kid in fifth grade._____

When? __Recess._____

What happened? ____I kept playing. The kid teased me more._____
_____Then he stopped._____

_____

How did I do?

Why did I circle this? _____I forgot to stop and count to five._____

_____

From *Skillstreaming the Elementary School Child–Student Manual,* by E. McGinnis &
A. P. Goldstein, 1997, Champaign IL: Research Press.

Skillstreaming the Elementary School Child
Parent/Staff Skill Rating Form

Date: _____

_____ is learning
(student's name)

the skill of _____

The steps involved in this skill are:

1. Did he or she demonstrate this skill in your presence? ☐ yes   ☐ no

2. How would you rate his or her skill demonstration? *(check one)*

   ☐ poor   ☐ below average   ☐ average   ☐ above average   ☐ excellent

3. How sincere was he or she in performing the skill? *(check one)*

   ☐ not sincere   ☐ somewhat sincere   ☐ very sincere

Comments: _____

_____

_____

_____

Please sign and return this form to _____

by _____

Signature: _____ Date: _____

From *Skillstreaming the Elementary School Child: New Strategies and Perspectives for Teaching Prosocial Skills–Program Forms* (Rev. Ed.), by E. McGinnis & A. P. Goldstein, 1997, Champaign IL: Research Press.

Skillstreaming the Elementary School Child
Teacher/Staff Skillstreaming Checklist

Student:_____ Class/age: _____

Teacher/staff: _____ Date: _____

INSTRUCTIONS: Listed below you will find a number of skills that children are more or less proficient in using. This checklist will help you evaluate how well each child uses the various skills. For each child, rate his/her use of each skill, based on your observations of the his/her behavior in various situations.

Circle 1 if the child is *almost never* good at using the skill.
Circle 2 if the child is *seldom* good at using the skill.
Circle 3 if the child is *sometimes* good at using the skill.
Circle 4 if the child is *often* good at using the skill.
Circle 5 if the child is *almost always* good at using the skill.

Please rate the child on all skills listed. If you know of a situation in which the child has particular difficulty in using the skill well, please note it briefly in the space marked "Problem situation."

	almost never	seldom	sometimes	often	almost always
1. **Listening:** Does the student appear to listen when someone is speaking and make an effort to understand what is said?	1	2	3	4	5

Problem situation:

2. **Asking for Help:** Does the student decide when he/she needs assistance and ask for this help in a pleasant manner?	1	2	3	4	5

Problem situation:

3. **Saying Thank You:** Does the student tell others he/she appreciates help given, favors, and so forth?	1	2	3	4	5

Problem situation:

From *Skillstreaming the Elementary School Child: New Strategies and Perspectives for Teaching Prosocial Skills–Program Forms* (Rev. Ed.), by E. McGinnis & A. P. Goldstein, 1997, Champaign IL: Research Press.

Skillstreaming in Early Childhood
Parent Skill Checklist

Name _____ Date _____

Child's Name _____ Birth Date _____

Directions: Based on your observations in various situations, rate your child's use of the
following skills.

Circle 1 if your child *almost never* uses the skill.
Circle 2 if your child *seldom* uses the skill.
Circle 3 if your child *sometimes* uses the skill.
Circle 4 if your child *often* uses the skill.
Circle 5 if your child *almost always* uses the skill.

	Almost never	Seldom	Sometimes	Often	Almost always
1. Does your child listen and understand when you or others talk to him/her?	1	2	3	4	5

Comments:

2. Does your child speak to others in a friendly manner?	1	2	3	4	5

Comments:

3. Does your child use a brave or assertive manner when in a conflict with another child?	1	2	3	4	5

Comments:

From *Skillstreaming in Early Childhood: Teaching Prosocial Skills to the Preschool and Kindergarten Child–Program Forms,* by E. McGinnis & A. P. Goldstein, 1990, Champaign IL: Research Press.

Skillstreaming the Elementary School Child
Student Skillstreaming Checklist

Name: _____ Date: _____

INSTRUCTIONS: Each of the questions will ask you about how well you do something. Next to each question is a number.

Circle number 1 if you *almost never* do what the question asks.
Circle number 2 if you *seldom* do it.
Circle number 3 if you *sometimes* do it.
Circle number 4 if you do it *often*.
Circle number 5 if you *almost always* do it.

There are no right or wrong answers to these questions.
Answer the way you really feel about each question.

	almost never	seldom	sometimes	often	almost always
1. Is it easy for me to listen to someone who is talking to me?	1	2	3	4	5
2. Do I ask for help in a friendly way when I need help?	1	2	3	4	5
3. Do I tell people thank you for something they have done for me?	1	2	3	4	5
4. Do I have the materials I need for my classes (like books, pencils, paper)?	1	2	3	4	5
5. Do I understand what to do when directions are given, and do I follow these directions?	1	2	3	4	5
6. Do I finish my schoolwork?	1	2	3	4	5
7. Do I join in on class talks or discussions?	1	2	3	4	5
8. Do I try to help an adult when I think he/she could use the help?	1	2	3	4	5
9. Do I decide what I don't understand about my schoolwork and ask my teacher questions in a friendly way?	1	2	3	4	5
10. Is it easy for me to keep doing my schoolwork when people are noisy?	1	2	3	4	5

From *Skillstreaming the Elementary School Child: New Strategies and Perspectives for Teaching Prosocial Skills–Program Forms* (Rev. Ed.), by E. McGinnis & A. P. Goldstein, 1997, Champaign IL: Research Press.

Skillstreaming the Adolescent
Skillstreaming Grouping Chart

	student names								
Group I: Beginning Social Skills									
1. Listening									
2. Starting a Conversation									
3. Having a Conversation									
4. Asking a Question									
5. Saying Thank You									
6. Introducing Yourself									
7. Introducing Other People									
8. Giving a Compliment									
Group II: Advanced Social Skills									
9. Asking for Help									
10. Joining In									
11. Giving Instructions									
12. Following Instructions									
13. Apologizing									
14. Convincing Others									
Group III: Skills for Dealing with Feelings									
15. Knowing Your Feelings									
16. Expressing Your Feelings									

From *Skillstreaming the Adolescent: New Strategies and Perspectives for Teaching Prosocial Skills–Program Forms*, by A. P. Goldstein & E. McGinnis, 1997, Champaign IL: Research Press.

Skillstreaming Arrangements

1. **Number of trainers: 2 per group preferable**

2. **Trainer-trainee cultural compatibility:**
   From same culture
   Trainer past experience

3. **Number of trainees: 6 to 8**

4. **Select and group to match trainees' real-life peers**

5. **Criterion for inclusion: skill deficiency**

6. **Criteria for exclusion:**
   Skill proficiency
   Severe attention deficit (after trial group)
   Severe generalization deficit (after trial group)

7. **Sessions per week: 2 optimal (15 minutes to 1½ hours)**

8. **Materials needed: skills cards, skill posters, flipchart/chalkboard**

9. **Placement in curriculum:**
   Homeroom   Social studies
   Resource room   English
   In-school suspension   Physical education
   After-school detention Life skills class

10. **Track criteria to assess effectiveness**

11. **Diffuse to entire school/district**

Effective In-School Suspension

1. Notify parents regarding cause, length, and remediation.

2. Employ certified teachers/proctors to supervise.

3. Require prosocial skills training targeted to remediate cause.

4. Require completion of all assigned class work from regular classes before return.

5. Allow no participation in extracurricular activities.

6. Require reentry conference with student and parents before return.

Part 2
Notes

Part 3
The Skillstreaming Setting: Creating Safe Schools

No intervention is any better than the context in which it is offered. For Skillstreaming to be effective, it must be offered in an environment free of intimidation, chaos, or aggression. Dr. Goldstein presents methods for establishing such an environment. He places particular emphasis on early interventions that "catch it low to prevent it high," discussing the importance of interventions for low-level forms of aggression, such as cursing, teasing, and bullying.

He also discusses interventions for high-level forms of aggression, highlighting such topics as breaking up student fights safely, physical school alterations that minimize violence, and predicting student violence. Dr. Goldstein closes with a segment on parent outreach strategies that will promote safe schools.

School violence and aggression are discussed in detail in the following publications:

Goldstein, A. P. (1996). *The psychology of vandalism*. New York: Plenum.

Goldstein, A. P. (1999). *Low-level aggression: First steps on the ladder to violence*. Champaign IL: Research Press.

Goldstein, A. P., Palumbo, J., Striepling, S., & Voutsinas, A. M. (1995). *Break it up: A teacher's guide to managing student aggression*. Champaign IL: Research Press.

Goldstein, A. P., Palumbo, J., & Striepling, S. (1995). *Break it up: Managing student fights* [Videotape]. Champaign IL: Research Press.

Goldstein, A. P., & Conoley, J. (Eds.). (1997). *School violence intervention: A practical handbook*. New York: Guilford.

Goldstein, A. P., & Kodluboy, D. W. (1998). *Gangs in schools: Signs, symbols, and solutions*. Champaign IL: Research Press.

Aggressive Incidents

- **Horseplay**
- **Rules violation**
- **Disruptiveness**
- **Refusal/defiance**
- **Cursing**
- **Bullying**
- **Sexual harassment**
- **Physical threats**
- **Vandalism**
- **Out-of-control behavior**
- **Student-student fights**
- **Attacks on teachers**
- **Use of weapons**
- **Collective violence**

From *Break It Up: A Teacher's Guide to Managing Student Aggression*, by A. P. Goldstein, J. Palumbo, S. Striepling, & A. M. Voutsinas, 1995, Champaign IL: Research Press.

Disruptive Student Behaviors on the School Bus

Low Levels
- Littering/eating/drinking
- Excessive noise
- Rules violation
- Out of seat
- Disturbing others

Medium Levels
- Profanity
- Refusal to obey driver
- Arm/body out of window
- Smoking
- Throwing objects

High Levels
- Destruction of property
- Pushing/tripping/attacking others
- Discriminatory language (includes sexual harassment)
- Attacks on driver
- Weapons
- Group attacks

From *Driving Me Crazy: School Transportation and Student Discipline,* by Trina Cron, 1998, Santa Fe NM: Goin' Mobile.

Motivations for Cursing

- **Aggression**

- **Rebellion**

- **Attention-seeking**

- **Imitation**

- **Impression management (to sound "tough")**

- **Preoccupation with body organs and sexual acts**

Interventions for Cursing

- **Extinction**

- **Instructed repetition**

- **Nonsense word substitution**

- **School/institution sanctions plus "Catch them being good"**

Teasing

- **Physical appearance (especially overweight)**

- **Intellectual performance (too slow or too smart)**

- **Physical and athletic performance**

- **Interest in opposite or same sex**

- **Personal hygiene**

- **Race**

- **Fearfulness**

- **Psychological problems**

- **Handicapping conditions**

Bullying Behaviors

- **Name-calling**

- **Physical attack**

- **Threatening**

- **Theft**

- **Spreading rumors**

- **Racial slurs**

- **Shunning**

Bullies and Their Victims

Bullies	Whipping Boys
Physically stronger	**Physically weaker**
Impulsive	**Cautious, quiet**
Broadly aggressive	**Withdrawn, with few friends**
High dominance needs	**Anxious, sensitive**
Low empathy	**See self as failure**

Participants in Bullying

1. **Bully**

2. **Victim**

3. **Outsider**
   (does nothing, ignores bullying, leaves)

4. **Reinforcer**
   (incites by shouting approval)

5. **Assistant**
   (joins in the bullying)

6. **Defender**
   (tells adult, comforts victims, attacks bully)

Interventions for Bullying

1. Create a "telling" school climate.

2. Use classroom brainstorming discussions.

3. Promote school-wide anti-bullying campaigns with posters.

4. Place on PTO/PTA agenda.

5. Initiate staff programs to help student "loners."

6. "Capture" the power needs of bullies.

7. Punish bullies.

8. Train victims in defusing skills.

9. Sensitize *all* staff to signs, locations, interventions.

Dealing with Sexual Harassment

- Develop and publicize a sexual harassment policy that explains what types of conduct will be considered sexual harassment.

- Develop and publicize a specific grievance procedure.

- Develop methods to inform staff and students of the school's sexual harassment policy and grievance procedure.

- Conduct periodic sexual harassment awareness training for all school staff.

- Conduct periodic age-appropriate sexual harassment awareness training for students.

- Survey students to find out whether any sexual harassment is occurring at the school.

- Conduct periodic sexual harassment awareness training for parents of elementary and secondary students.

Characteristics of
High Vandalism-Prone Locations

- **Low surveillance**
- **Previously vandalized**
- **Public**
- **Newer**
- **Previously damaged (not vandalized)**

Weapons

Guns

Knives

Screwdrivers

Mace

Pens/pencils

Bats

Rocks

Bottles

Brass knuckles

Large rings

Two and three finger rings

Scissors

Stun guns

Chairs

Heavy belt buckles

Heavy false gold chains

Box cutters

Pen guns

Auto batons

Weighted gloves

Ammonia-filled spray bottles

Staples

Padlocks

Metal nail files

Steelies (in a bag)

Nunchukas

Slap jacks

Bayonets

Predicting Student Violence:
The Person

Thinking (Cognition)

- **Preoccupied with aggression**

  Talks, reads, watches TV, plays video
  games, writes graffiti

Feeling (Affect)

- **Anger**

  Frequent
  Easily provoked

- **Depression**

Doing (Behavior)

- **Aggressive acts**

  Frequent
  Intense
  Diverse (high and low level)
  Early onset

- **Seeks aggressive peers**

Predicting Student Violence: The Environment

- **Presence of weapons**
- **Parental aggression**
- **Parental mismanagement**
- **Peer aggression**
- **Peer isolation**
- **School climate**
  - **Frequent fights**
  - **Low surveillance**
  - **Insufficient bonding opportunities**
  - **Unmonitored, unauthorized persons**
  - **Inadequate security**

Environmental Interventions

- **Metal detectors**

- **Locker removal**

- **Locker/car search**

- **Locker sharing (student/faculty)**

- **Locker placement (opposite school office)**

- **Clear or mesh bookbags**

- **Weapon hotline**

- **Student photo ID**

Ecology of the Minimal Aggression Classroom

- ## Door
  Solid unbreakable window

  Inside lock

- ## Teacher Desk
  Bolted

  Placed to aid surveillance and escape

- ## Student Desks
  Bolted to floor

  Vandalism resistant

- ## Aisles
  Traffic-friendly

- ## Windows
  Plexiglass or polycarbon

  Grillwork covered

- ## Supplies
  In locked cabinet

  Removed if potential as weapon

Physical School Alterations

- Extensive lighting program

- Reduction of school size

- Reduction of class size

- Closing off isolated areas

- Increased staff supervision

- Implementation of rapid repair of vandalism targets

- Electronic monitoring for weapons detection

- Removal of tempting vandalism targets

- Installation of recessed fixtures where possible

- Installation of graffiti boards

- Encouragement of student-drawn murals

- Painting lockers bright colors

- Use of ceramic-type, hard-surface paints

- Sponsoring clean-up, pick-up, fix-up days

Physical School Alterations, cont.

- Paved or asphalt graveled parking areas

- Use of plexiglass or polycarbon windows

- Installation of decorative grillwork over windows

- Marking all school property for identification

- Open and observable school buildings

- Preventive custodial maintenance

- Use of intruder detectors (microwave, ultrasonic, infrared, audio, video, mechanical)

- Altering of isolated areas to attract people traffic

- Limited roof access

- Drainpipes covered to deter climbing

- No ledges on building or trees near building

- Trees/shrubs trimmed for surveillance

- School grounds free of gravel

- Student and faculty parking mixed

Environmental Design Methods

1. **Target hardening**
   (security screens, slash-proof seats)

2. **Access control**
   (locked doors, blocked-off streets)

3. **Deflecting offenders**
   (graffiti boards, home activity decoys)

4. **Controlling facilitators**
   (spray can sales control, plastic "glass")

5. **Entry/exit screening**
   (closed-circuit TV, merchandise tags)

6. **Formal surveillance**
   (burglar alarms, tenant patrols)

7. **Employee surveillance**
   (aisle mirrors, more employees)

8. **Natural surveillance**
   (improved lighting, clear store windows)

9. **Target removal**
   (exact change fares, removable car radios)

10. **Identifying property**
    (vehicle parts ID, property marking with SS #)

11. **Removing inducements**
    (rapid graffiti cleaning, small window panes)

12. **Rule setting**
    (drug-free school zones, building design codes)

Interventions for Bystanders and Witnesses to Violence

- **Acknowledge that the violent event occurred**

- **Provide a respite time and place**

- **Provide extended opportunities to:**
  - Talk
  - Cry
  - Grieve
  - Express anxiety

- **Publicize efforts to prevent reoccurrence and increase safety**

- **Enlist assistance in accomplishing all of the above from:**
  - All school personnel
  - Parents
  - Peers
  - Community figures (police, clergy, etc.)

Significant Correlates of Exposure to Violence

- Increased anxiety

- Increased fearfulness

- Depressed mood

- Decreased energy

- Sleep disturbances

- Appetite disturbance

- Impaired cognitive functioning

- Increased hostility

Interventions for Classroom Survivors

- Attend funeral or memorial service as desired.

- Give students, parents, and school staff opportunities to talk to a reassuring adult about fears, anger, sorrow.

- Give students, parents, and school staff opportunities to talk to each other about fears, anger, sorrow.

- Arrange early return to routine and, if desired, to site of event.

- Offer availability of mental health specialists.

- Offer relevant information.
  Rarity of school violence
  Security measures being taken
  Normality of grieving process

- Monitor for long-term effects.

Managing the Fight Scene

1. **Make a quick assessment.**

    Consider disputants, weapons, need for assistance.

2. **Call for help.**

3. **Use defusing tactics.**

    Model calmness, talk softly and slowly, call students by name, use requests or distraction.

    Avoid threats, ridicule, running, physical proximity, interposing self between students.

4. **Separate students only if you are skilled and safe.**

5. **Control crowd.**

6. **Interview disputants.**

7. **Take appropriate action.**

    Consider counseling, mediation, referral, suspension, call to parents, call to police.

8. **Debrief class.**

9. **Care for self.**

From *Break It Up: A Teacher's Guide to Managing Student Aggression*, by A. P. Goldstein, J. Palumbo, S. Striepling, & A. M. Voutsinas, 1995, Champaign IL: Research Press.

Crowd Control

1. Try to form a perimeter around the fight scene.

2. Speak to gathering students in a non-threatening but assertive tone.

3. Make statements that reassure the crowd.

    "Everything is okay."
    "You can help these people out by going to your classroom."
    "Go to your rooms."

4. Be prepared to block students' paths or view, if you are able.

5. Close corridor doors if possible.

6. Redirect hall traffic to other routes.

7. Be prepared to call for more assistance if needed.

From *Break It Up: A Teacher's Guide to Managing Student Aggression*, by A. P. Goldstein, J. Palumbo, S. Striepling, & A. M. Voutsinas, 1995, Champaign IL: Research Press.

Handling Angry Parents

1. Schedule conferences in advance.

2. Set and communicate procedures to avoid class disruption or school building "ambush."

3. If difficulty is expected:
   Do not meet in isolated areas.
   Ask another staff member to sit in.
   Leave room door slightly ajar.

4. Listen respectfully.

5. Stay calm.

6. Show understanding.

7. Help save face.

8. Seek win-win solution.

Parent Outreach Strategies

1. Include parent representatives on school safety and school improvement committees.

2. Send copy of school's discipline code to all parents and seek their support of it.

3. Create parent telephone network to encourage parent attendance at school events.

4. Establish School-Home Note Program concerning accomplishments, behavior, etc.

5. Use parent volunteers as tutors, aides, safety patrol, etc.

6. Establish and promote parent adopt-a-school programs.

Part 3
Notes

Part 4
Skillstreaming: Reducing Resistance, Increasing Motivation, and Enhancing Generalization

Problems can and do occur in the Skillstreaming group. In this video, Dr. Goldstein presents means to prevent or reduce group management problems, such as inactivity, hyperactivity, active resistance, and aggression. He then continues with a discussion of how to motivate trainees to attend and participate productively in the Skillstreaming group. Dr. Goldstein emphasizes the importance of negotiating the curriculum with the trainees so that they will understand the relevance of the skills in their everyday lives.

Dr. Goldstein discusses effective procedures for promoting generalization of the skills learned in the group to school, home, and community settings. He closes his presentation with comments on the importance of a systems-based approach and ways to increase school/home collaboration.

The following videotapes—for student viewing—are designed to enhance motivation and reduce resistance during group training sessions:

Goldstein, A. P., & McGinnis, E. (1997). *People skills: Doing 'em right!—Adolescent level* [Videotape]. Champaign IL: Research Press.

McGinnis, E., & Goldstein, A. P. (1997). *People skills: Doing 'em right!—Elementary level* [Videotape]. Champaign IL: Research Press.

Types of Group Management Problems

Inactivity
- Minimal participation
- Apathy
- Falling asleep

Hyperactivity
- Digression
- Monopolizing
- Interruption
- Excessive restlessness

Active Resistance
- Participation, but not as instructed
- Passive-aggressive isolation
- Negativism, refusal
- Disruptiveness

Aggression
- Sarcasm, put-downs
- Bullying, intimidation
- Use of threats
- Assaultiveness

Cognitive Inadequacies and Emotional Disturbances
- Inability to pay attention
- Inability to understand
- Inability to remember
- Bizarre behavior

From *Skillstreaming the Adolescent: New Strategies and Perspectives for Teaching Prosocial Skills* (Rev. Ed.), by A. P. Goldstein & E. McGinnis, 1997, Champaign IL: Research Press.

Methods for Reducing Group Management Problems

Simplification Methods
- Reward minimal trainee accomplishment.
- Shorten the role-play.
- Have trainer "feed" sentences to the trainee.
- Have trainee read a prepared script portraying the behavioral steps.
- Have trainee play co-actor role first.

Threat-Reduction Methods
- Employ additional live modeling by the trainers.
- Postpone trainee's role-playing until last in sequence.
- Provide reassurance to the trainee.
- Provide empathic encouragement to the trainee.
- Clarify aspects of the trainee's task which are experienced as threatening.
- Restructure aspects of the trainee's task which are experienced as threatening.

Termination of Response Methods
- Interrupt ongoing trainee behavior.
- Ignore ongoing trainee behavior.
- Discontinue contact and turn to another trainee.
- Remove trainee from group participation.

From *Skillstreaming the Adolescent: New Strategies and Perspectives for Teaching Prosocial Skills* (Rev. Ed.), by A. P. Goldstein & E. McGinnis, 1997, Champaign IL: Research Press.

Behavior Modification Procedures to Reduce Aggression

- **Behavioral rules**

- **Removing positive reinforcers**
  Extinction
  Time out
  Response cost

- **Presenting positive reinforcers**

- **Overcorrection**
  Restitution plus positive practice

- **Contingency contracting**

Rules for Rules

- **Few in number**

- **Negotiated with students**

- **Behaviorally stated**

- **Positively stated**

- **Posted in classroom**

- **Contracted with youth and parents**

Do Not Lose Your Bus Privilege
Follow These Rules

- Keep belongings in bookbag.

- Use caution when approaching, entering, and exiting the bus.

- Show respect to other students and the driver.

- Help others, when needed.

- Follow the driver's directions.

- Talk with the driver when problems arise.

- Yield to other students without pushing.

- Stay in your seat.

- Keep arms, head, and body in the bus at all times.

- Do not:
    yell
    push other students
    throw objects
    use unacceptable language
    destroy property
    fight

Good Rider Awards

- **The breakfast club**
  (every other month, 6 students per bus)

- **Award certificates**

- **Ribbons, badges, stickers**

- **Magnets, pens, pencils**

- **Listing in local newspaper "Good Rider" column**

- **Fast-food restaurant certificates**

Skillstreaming Skill Checklist Choices

Skill	Number of persons choosing it
Dealing with an accusation	6
Keeping out of fights	4
Dealing with group pressure	4
Responding to anger	3
Expressing a complaint	1
Responding to failure	0

Generalization Strategies

1. Increase quantity of the intervention.

2. Increase quality of the intervention.

3. Increase system support and reciprocity.

4. Build more potent interventions.

Skill Sequence

Skill 42: Dealing with Group Pressure

1. Think about what the group wants you to do and why.

2. Decide what you want to do.

3. Decide how to tell the group what you want to do.

4. Tell the group what you have decided.

Skill 38: Responding to Failure

1. Decide if you have failed at something.

2. Think about why you failed.

3. Think about what you could do to keep from failing another time.

4. Decide if you want to try again.

5. Try again using your new idea.

Skill 27: Standing Up for Your Rights

1. Pay attention to what is going on in your body that helps you know that you are dissatisfied and would like to stand up for yourself.

2. Decide what happened to make you feel dissatisfied.

3. Think about ways in which you might stand up for yourself and choose one.

4. Stand up for yourself in a direct and reasonable way.

Generalization Enhancement: Transfer

1. **Provision of general principles (general case programming)**

2. **Overlearning (maximizing response availability)**

3. **Stimulus variability (training sufficient exemplars, training loosely)**

4. **Identical elements (programming common stimuli)**

5. **Mediated generalization (self-recording, self-reinforcement, self-punishment, self-instruction)**

6. **Sequential modification**

Generalization Enhancement: Maintenance

1. Thinning reinforcement (increasing intermittency, unpredictability)

2. Delaying reinforcement

3. Fading prompts

4. Booster sessions

5. Preparing for natural nonreinforcement

   Teach self-reinforcement.
   Teach relapse and failure management skills.
   Use graduated homework assignments.

6. Programming for reinforcement in the natural environment

7. Using natural reinforcers

   Observe real-life settings.
   Indentify easily reinforced behaviors.
   Teach reinforcement recruitment.
   Teach reinforcement recognition.

Systems Approach

- **Parents**
- **Peers**
- **Siblings**
- **Teachers**
- **School administrators**
- **Community figures:**
    Religious
    Business
    Agency
    Police
    Probation
    Others

Barriers to School/Home Collaboration

School Initiated

1. Separation, "bake sale," adversarial, and blaming traditions

2. Professional dominance attitude, rather than person to person

3. Time constraints

4. Structural constraints (vehicles and venues)

Parent Initiated

1. Time constraints

2. Job and family demands

3. Transportation, baby sitters

4. Differing cultural backgrounds (language, achievement expectations, role of teacher)

5. School conferences as "bad news" meetings only

Immigrant Families:
Issues in Home/School Collaboration

- **Differing cultural expectations of parental roles (disengagement-involvement)**

- **Teacher as ultimate authority or as racist authority**

- **Limited English proficiency**

- **Limited time availability**

- **Fear due to lack of appropriate documentation**

Sample Letter to Parents

Dear Mrs. Smith,

I am Susan Striepling, Jason's social studies teacher. I want to welcome you and your son, Jason, to my class for this school year. I am looking forward to a great year and I hope Jason is also.

Social Studies this year, as mandated by the state of New York, will cover American History from the founding to the present. We have a lot to cover and we'll be moving fairly fast, so I hope that Jason will make every effort to keep up. If, at any time, he is having problems, he will need to see me right away so we can be sure he doesn't fall behind. I am usually available every day after school for extra help. He should check with me in class to be sure I don't have a school meeting on the day he plans to come.

I try to keep my classroom rules as simple as possible. They are all related to helping the classroom be the best learning environment as possible for everyone. The basic ones are: Speak in a positive manner about yourself and others; keep your hands, arms, feet, head, and any other parts of your body in your own space; speak in class only when it is your turn and then in a manner that shows you respect yourself, your teacher, and your peers; turn all your work in on time done in a way that makes you proud of yourself.

There are certain classroom procedures, which help to make the class run as smoothly as possible, such as when to use the lavatory, when to sharpen pencils, where to put completed homework, etc. We are in the process of learning these now in class.

I expect homework to be turned in on the day it is assigned, unless Jason has been out sick or I have spoken with you. I do not assign busy work. What Jason has for homework will help him be successful on tests and quizzes in class. I give a short quiz each Friday at the beginning of class which reviews the work we have done that week. Tests are given as we complete each unit. If Jason is doing his classwork and homework, he should not have difficulty on these tests and quizzes. If Jason receives less than 70% on a test or quiz, he may correct the test or quiz, after school. If his corrections are 100%, I will then raise his test or quiz grade to 85%. Therefore, if Jason is turning in his homework, doing his journal and special projects, and participating in class, there is no reason for him not to receive a passing grade. My grades are figured as follows: 20% homework, 50% tests and quizes, 20% special projects (includes a class journal), 10% class participation.

We will be doing two major research projects this year, one in the fall and one in the spring. These will involve library research which we will be doing during class time, home interviews, a graphics component, and a final paper. I will be sending a more detailed description home to you at the time we do this project, with suggestions on how you can help Jason be successful with his project.

Mrs. Smith, one of the most important things which will contribute to Jason's having a successful year in social studies is for you and me to stay in close contact about what is going on in schcol and what is going on at home. Please call me with any concerns you have. You can reach me at the school (555-2345) during the school day. Please leave a message and I will get back to you that afternoon, after the students leave, or that evening from home.

I'm looking forward to meeting you soon and having a great year with Jason.

Sincerely yours,

Susan Striepling

Skillstreaming the Adolescent
School-Home Note

Student:_____ Date: _____

DESCRIPTION OF LESSON

Skill name: _____

Skill steps:

Skill purpose, use, value: _____

_____

DESCRIPTION OF SKILL HOMEWORK

_____

_____

REQUEST TO PARENTS

1. Provide skill homework recognition and reward.

2. Provide skill homework reciprocation.

3. Return this School-Home Note with your comments (on the back) about:
   - Quality of homework done
   - Rewards that work/don't work at home
   - Suggestions or questions regarding this skill, other skills, additional homework assignments, other ways to promote school-home collaboration, and so on

4. Please sign and return this form to _____

   by _____

Signature: _____ Date: _____

From *Skillstreaming the Adolescent: New Strategies and Perspectives for Teaching Prosocial Skills–Program Forms,* by A. P. Goldstein & E. McGinnis, 1997, Champaign IL: Research Press.

Aggression Prevention and Control
Administration-Relevant Initiatives

1. Principal visibility and availability to teachers and students

2. Principal/administration support of teachers

3. Fair and consistent response to teacher or student grievances

4. Fair and consistent rule enforcement

5. Clear lines of responsibility among administrators and between administrators and teachers

6. Effective intelligence network

7. Ethnic knowledge/sensitivity/skill training for teachers

8. Aggression management training for teachers

9. School safety committee

10. Legal rights handbook/school procedure manual

11. Code of rights and responsibilities

12. Community outreach programming

Aggression Prevention and Control
Teacher-Relevant Initiatives

1. Low teacher-pupil ratio

2. Classroom arrangement
   (desk placed to surveil, escape, roam)

3. Rules: few, negotiated, defined, positive,
   enforceable, contracted, posted

4. Firm, fair, consistent discipline

5. Consistently optimistic academic
   expectations

6. Curricula content of high "real-world"
   relevance

7. Teacher-as-protector to provide risk-
   taking security

8. Individualized teaching strategies

9. Ethnic knowledge/sensitivity/skill training
   for teachers

10. Aggression management training for teachers

11. Teacher-student class meetings
    (on rules, problems, curriculum)

12. Teacher-student nonclass contact

13. Teacher-parent collaboration

Teachers as Violence Enablers

- **Avoiding high-violence school locations**

- **Ignoring student complaints of being threatened**

- **Ignoring low-level violence: put downs, bullying, harassment**

- **Ignoring student threats of planned violence**

- **Ignoring rumors about students who may have a weapon**

- **Failing to intervene or report witnessed student violence**

- **Excusing violent behavior of "good kids" as necessary for self-defense**

From *Violence in Schools: The Enabling Factor*, by C. Remboldt, 1994, Minneapolis: Johnson Institute.

Unauthorized Persons
on School Property

- **Prepare and provide visitor regulation list.**

- **Limit and monitor visitor entry and movement.**

- **Use ID system for students.**

- **Require visitor sign-in and badges.**

- **Install alarms on rarely used doors.**

- **Register and sticker all staff and student cars.**

- **Establish closed campus policy (student sign in and out during day).**

- **Question and discourage loiterers.**

Part 4
Notes

Part 5
Aggression Replacement Training

Skillstreaming teaches youth what to do instead of aggression. When youth fail to use the prosocial skills they have learned in the Skillstreaming group, it is often because they are too emotionally primed, too well rehearsed in aggressive responding, and/or too committed to immature, egocentric, antisocial values. Aggression Replacement Training addresses each of these concerns in its three coordinated components: Skillstreaming (the behavioral component) — teaches what to do, Anger Control Training (the emotional component) — teaches what not to do, and Moral Reasoning Training (the values component) — teaches why to use the skills.

Dr. Goldstein discusses the rationale and training procedures for Anger Control Training, which is designed to serve two related purposes: (1) to help make the arousal of anger in aggressive youth a less frequent occurrence and (2) to provide them with the means to use self-control when their anger is aroused. He continues with a discussion of Moral Reasoning Training, which involves social decision making meetings in which the group leader presents problem situations (or moral dilemmas) and facilitates the development of more mature moral reasoning.

Anger Control Training and Moral Reasoning Training are discussed in detail in the following publications:

Gibbs, J. C., Potter, G. B., & Goldstein, A. P. (1995). *The EQUIP program: Teaching youth to think and act responsibly through a peer-helping approach*. Champaign IL: Research Press.

Goldstein, A. P., Glick, B., & Gibbs, J. C. (1998). *Aggression Replacement Training: A comprehensive intervention for aggressive youth* (rev. ed.). Champaign IL: Research Press.

Aggression Replacement Training

1. **Skillstreaming
   (the behavioral component)**
   > Teaches what to do—
   > the skills curriculum

2. **Anger Control Training
   (the emotional component)**
   > Teaches what not to do—
   > reduces anger, aggression

3. **Moral Reasoning Training
   (the values component)**
   > Teaches why to use the skills—
   > increases prosocial motivation

Hassle Log

Name: _____ Date: _____

☐ Morning   ☐ Afternoon   ☐ Evening

Where were you?

☐ Classroom   ☐ Bathroom   ☐ Off grounds

☐ Dorm   ☐ Team office   ☐ Hall

☐ Gym   ☐ Dining room   ☐ On a job

☐ Recreation room   ☐ Outside/grounds   ☐ Other

What happened?

☐ Somebody teased me.

☐ Somebody took something of mine.

☐ Somebody was doing something I didn't like.

☐ I did something wrong.

☐ Somebody started fighting with me.

☐ Other

Who was the other person?

☐ Another youth   ☐ Aide   ☐ Teacher   ☐ Counselor   ☐ Other

What did you do?

☐ Hit back   ☐ Told peer or adult

☐ Ran away   ☐ Ignored it

☐ Yelled   ☐ Used anger control technique

☐ Cried   _____

☐ Walked away calmly   _____

☐ Broke something   ☐ Talked it out

☐ Was restrained   ☐ Used Skillstreaming skill *(identify)*

☐ Told aide or counselor   _____

How angry were you?

☐ Burning   ☐ Really angry   ☐ Moderately angry   ☐ Mildly angry but still OK   ☐ Not angry at all

How did you handle yourself?

1	2	3	4	5
Poorly	Not so well	OK	Good	Great

From *Aggression Replacement Training: A Comprehension Intervention for Aggressive Youth* (Rev. Ed.), by A. P. Goldstein, B. Glick, & J. C. Gibbs, 1998, Champaign IL: Research Press.

Nonreader's Hassle Log

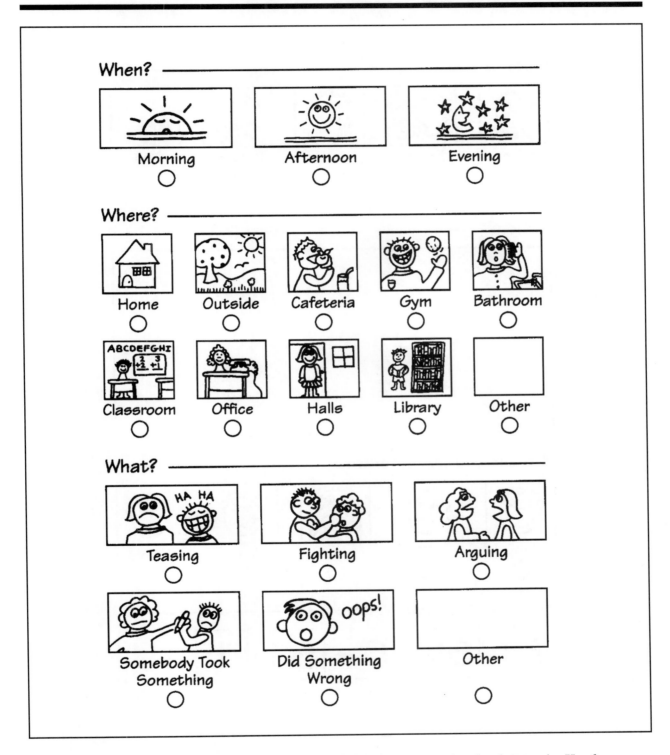

From *Aggression Replacement Training: A Comprehensive Intervention for Aggressive Youth* (Rev. Ed.), by A. P. Goldstein, B. Glick, & J. C. Gibbs, 1998, Champaign IL: Research Press. A personal communication to the authors from J. Gilliam.

Nonreader's Hassle Log, cont.

Who?

Friend	Parent	Teacher	Brother or Sister	Other
○	○	○	○	○

Action?

How did you feel afterwards?

Happy	OK	Sad	Mad	Scared
○	○	○	○	○

How did you handle yourself?

E	S⁺	S	S⁻	I	U
○	○	○	○	○	○

Anger Control Training

Triggers

1. External
2. Internal

+

Cues

+

Reducers

1. Deep breathing
2. Backward counting
3. Pleasant imagery
4. Thinking ahead

+

Reminders

+

Self-Evaluation

+

Skillstreaming Skill Use

From *Aggression Replacement Training: A Comprehensive Intervention for Aggressive Youth* (Rev. Ed.), by A. P. Goldstein, B. Glick, & J. C. Gibbs, 1998, Champaign IL: Research Press.

Anger Control Reminders

1. Preparing for Provocation

- I can manage this.
- Try not to take this too seriously.
- I know how to control my anger.

2. Impact and Confrontation

- Stay calm; just continue to relax.
- As long as I keep my cool, I'm in control.
- I'm not going to let him get to me.

3. Coping with Arousal

- Time to take a deep breath.
- My anger is a signal of what I need to do.
- Let's take the issue point by point.

4. Reflecting on the Provocation

- Try to shake it off; don't let it interfere.
- I handled that one pretty well.
- I'm doing better at this all the time.

From *Anger Control: The Development and Evaluation of an Experimental Treatment*, by R. W. Novaco, 1975, Lexington MA: D. C. Heath.

Reminder Categories

1. Cool Thoughts

- Just stay cool.
- This battle isn't worth it.

2. Problem-Solving Thoughts

- Okay, develop a plan.
- What's the first thing I want to do?

3. Control and Escape Thoughts

- I can always just walk away.
- It's okay to take time out.

4. Self-Rewarding Thoughts

- Good; I'm hanging in there.
- I feel great; I'm dealing with it and not yelling.

From "Cognitive-Behavioral Approaches to Anger Reduction," by J. L. Deffenbacher. In K. S. Dobson & K. D. Craig (Eds.), *Advances in Cognitive-Behavior Therapy*, 1996, Thousand Oaks CA: Sage.

Anger-Arousing Thinking Errors

1. Self-Centeredness

How dare he look at me that way!

2. Attribution of Hostile Intent

He's trying to make me look like a wimp.

3. Mislabeling

I have to defend myself.

4. Assuming the Worst

If I don't smack him, I am a wimp.

5. Blaming Others

He's asking for it. I'll do it.

From *The EQUIP Program: Teaching Youth to Think and Act Responsibly Through a Peer-Helping Approach*, by J. C. Gibbs, G. B. Potter, & A. P. Goldstein, 1995, Champaign IL: Research Press.

General Cognitive Restructuring Strategies for Self-Instruction Training

1. Question the evidence.

2. Dispute irrational beliefs (e.g., hostile intent of others).

3. Redirect attention to nonhostile cues.

4. Decatastrophize (what is the worst that can happen?).

5. Examine options and alternatives: generate several solutions.

6. Generate assertive rather than aggressive responses.

7. Reduce imaginal ruminating about the anger-inducing event.

8. Reduce imaginal exaggeration of the anger-inducing event.

9. Consider both short- and long-term consequences of both aggressive and prosocial responses.

10. Plan and rehearse prosocial response, step by step.

Dilemma Discussion Group Format

1. Create or reiterate proper set.

2. Hand out and read dilemma.

3. Summarize major points.

4. Obtain member opinions: solutions and reasoning.

5. Obtain hand vote regarding solutions.

6. Divide members into two groups.

7. Separate groups, one trainer to each.

8. Help each group develop best reason(s) for their position.

9. Have each group elect a spokesperson.

10. Have each spokesperson present position (list on chalkboard).

11. Guide the two groups in debate.

12. End debate when views converge or exposure complete.

Moral Reasoning Training

1. Before meeting have youths read problem situation and respond to its questions.

2. Prepare table of responses. Enter responses and tentative majority decisions.

3. Open the meeting:

   - Give members back their problem situation responses.

   - Discuss problem situation to be sure it is understood and they see personal relevance.

     > What is the problem?
     > Why is it a problem?
     > Do problems like this really happen?
     > Who has been in a situation like this?

   - Display table of responses.

4. Elicit, discuss, and list mature reasoning from group members.

   > Goal: Highlight, cultivate.

5. Elicit, discuss, and list immature reasoning from group members.

   Invite mature reasoners to respond.

   > Goal: Remediate moral development delay, reduce egocentric bias.
   >
   > > What would the world be like if everyone did that?
   > > What should (person 1) do from (person 2's) point of view?
   > > How would you feel if you were _____?

6. Consolidate mature morality.

   > Goal: Seek unanimous mature final reasoning and decisions.

From *Aggression Replacement Training: A Comprehensive Intervention for Aggressive Youth* (Rev. Ed.), by A. P. Goldstein, B. Glick, & J. C. Gibbs, 1998, Champaign IL: Research Press.

Jerry's Problem Situation

Jerry had just moved to a new school and was feeling pretty lonely until one day a guy named Bob came up and introduced himself. "Hi, Jerry. My name is Bob. I heard one of the teachers say you're new here. If you're not doing anything after school today, how about coming over to shoot some baskets?" Pretty soon Jerry and Bob were good friends.

One day when Jerry was shooting baskets by himself, the basketball coach saw him and invited him to try out for the team. Jerry made the team, and every day after school he would practice with the rest of the team. After practice, Jerry and his teammates would always go out together to get something to eat and sit around and talk about stuff. On weekends they would sometimes take trips together.

As Jerry spends more time with the team, he sees less and less of Bob, his old friend. One day, Jerry gets a call from Bob. "Say, I was wondering," says Bob, "if you're not too busy on Thursday, my family is having a little birthday party for me. Maybe you could come over for dinner that night." Jerry tells Bob he'll try to come to the party. But during practice on Thursday, everyone tells Jerry about the great place they're all going to after practice.

What should Jerry say or do?

1. **Should Jerry go with the team?**

   go with team / go to Bob's party / can't decide *(circle one)*

2. **What if Jerry calls Bob from school and says he's sorry, but something has come up and he can't come over after all? Then would it be all right for Jerry to go with the team?**

   go with team / go to Bob's party / can't decide *(circle one)*

3. **What if Jerry considers that his teammates may be upset if Jerry doesn't come—that they may start to think Jerry's not such a good friend? Then would it be all right for Jerry to go with the team?**

   go with team / go to Bob's party / can't decide *(circle one)*

From *Aggression Replacement Training: A Comprehensive Intervention for Aggressive Youth* (Rev. Ed.), by A. P. Goldstein, B. Glick, & J. C. Gibbs, 1998, Champaign IL: Research Press.

Jerry's Problem Situation, cont.

4. What if Jerry thinks that, after all, Bob came along and helped Jerry when Jerry was lonely. Then should Jerry go with the team?

   go with team / go to Bob's party / can't decide *(circle one)*

5. Let's change the situation a bit. Let's say that before Bob asks Jerry to come over, the teammates ask if Jerry will be coming along on Thursday. Jerry says he thinks so. Then Bob asks Jerry. Then what should Jerry do?

   go with team / go to Bob's party / can't decide *(circle one)*

6. Which is more important: to have one close friend or to have a group of regular friends?

   one close friend / group of regular friends / can't decide *(circle one)*

7. Let's change the situation a different way. What if Jerry and Bob are not good friends but instead are just acquaintances? Then should Jerry go with the team?

   go with team / go to Bob's party / can't decide *(circle one)*

Responses to Jerry's Problem Situation

Name	Question Number						
	1	2	3	4	5	6	7
Dante	party	team	party	party	team	close friend	team
David	team	team	team	party	team	close friend	team
Tommy	can't decide	party	team	party	team	close friend	can't decide
Robert	party	party	party	party	can't decide	close friend	team
Andy	team	team	team	team	team	can't decide	team
Daniel	party	party	party	party	team	close friend	team
Earl	party	party	party	party	party	close friend	party
Jonathan	party	party	party	party	party	close friend	team
Brian	party	party	party	party	party	close friend	party
Group decision:	Bob's party?	Bob's party?	Bob's party?	Bob's party?	go with team?	close friend?	go with team?

Possible Group Decision Outcomes

Group decision: Bob's party	Bob's party	Bob's party	Bob's party	go with team?	close friend	go with team?

Aggression Replacement Training Program Implementation

1. **Master trainer selection**

2. **Trainer selection**

3. ***Aggression Replacement Training* text distributed to all involved personnel**

4. **Trainee selection**

5. **Motivation campaign**

6. **Skill curriculum negotiation**

7. **Program initiation**

8. **Master trainer observation and monitoring**

9. **Peer trainer supervision**

10. **Continued trainer/trainee motivation**

11. **The Transfer Coach**

12. **Assessment of trainee skill competency and consequences**

Optimal Qualities of the Aggression Replacement Training Trainer

1. Procedural knowledge of Aggression Replacement Training

2. Pedagogical skills
   a. With-it-ness awareness
   b. Overlapping two or more events
   c. Smoothness in transitions
   d. Instructing with momentum
   e. Communicating positive expectancies
   f. Maintaining group focus

3. Group facilitation skills
   a. Structuring
   b. Motivating
   c. Managing resistance
   d. Dramaturgical

4. Comfort with adolescents/children

5. Model of social skills, anger control, mature morality

6. Generalization enhancement skills

7. Administrative/organizational skills

   Irrelevant:
   Credentials, occupation
   Age, gender

Part 5
Notes

Part 6
The Prepare Curriculum and Antisocial Youth: Productive and Unproductive Intervention Strategies

In the first segment of this video, Dr. Goldstein discusses the Prepare Curriculum. As an extension of Skillstreaming and Aggression Replacement Training, the Prepare Curriculum provides interventions for training aggressive youth in such areas as problem-solving, empathy, stress management, and cooperation. Dr. Goldstein traces the development of this comprehensive, ten-course curriculum; discusses its rationale; and presents examples of training activities from the Prepare courses.

In the second segment, Dr. Goldstein offers a series of valuable criteria for evaluating the effectiveness of intervention strategies with aggressive youth. He analyzes why some commonly used strategies actually prove to be unproductive. He then discusses strategies that can lead to effective interventions with aggressive youth and provides guidelines for selecting techniques that follow from these intervention strategies.

The ten-course Prepare Curriculum is presented in:

Goldstein, A. P. (1999). *The Prepare Curriculum: Teaching prosocial competencies* (rev. ed.). Champaign IL: Research Press.

Psychoeducational Interventions: Developmental Progression

1973–1983	1984–1988	1988–Present
Skillstreaming	*Aggression Replacement Training*	*The Prepare Curriculum*
	1. Skillstreaming	1. Skillstreaming
	2. Anger Control Training	2. Anger Control Training
	3. Moral Reasoning Training	3. Moral Reasoning Training
		4. Problem-Solving Training
		5. Empathy Training
		6. Situational Perception Training
		7. Stress Management
		8. Cooperation Training
		9. Recruiting Supportive Models
		10. Understanding and Using Groups

The Prepare Curriculum

1. **Skillstreaming**

2. **Anger Control Training**

3. **Moral Reasoning Training**

4. **Problem-Solving Training**

5. **Empathy Training**

6. **Situational Perception Training**

7. **Stress Management Training**

8. **Cooperation Training**

9. **Recruiting Supportive Models**

10. **Understanding and Using Groups**

From *The Prepare Curriculum: Teaching Prosocial Competencies* (Rev. Ed.), by A. P. Goldstein, 1999, Champaign IL: Research Press.

The Prepare Curriculum: Problem-Solving Training

Session 1   Introduction

Session 2   Stop and Think

Session 3   Problem Identification

Session 4   Gathering Information (Own Perspective)

Session 5   Gathering Information (Others' Perspectives)

Session 6   Alternatives

Session 7   Evaluating Consequences and Outcomes

Session 8   Practice

From *The Prepare Curriculum: Teaching Prosocial Competencies* (Rev. Ed.), by A. P. Goldstein, 1999, Champaign IL: Research Press.

The Prepare Curriculum: Empathy Training

1. **Readiness Training**
   - Acquisition of empathy preparation skills
   - Elimination of empathy skill acquisition inhibitors

2. **Perceptual Training**
   - Situational perception training
   - Programmed self-instruction
   - Observational sensitivity training

3. **Affective Reverberation Training**
   - Meditation
   - Rolfing
   - Reichian therapy
   - Bioenergetics
   - Alexander technique
   - Feldenkrais' awareness through movement
   - Dance therapy
   - Sensory awareness training
   - Focusing
   - Laban-Bartenieff method

4. **Cognitive Analysis Training**
   - Discrimination training
   - Exposure plus guided practice

5. **Communication Training**
   - Didactic-experiential training
   - Interpersonal living laboratory
   - Relationship enhancement
   - Microtraining

6. **Transfer and Maintenance Training**

From *The Prepare Curriculum: Teaching Prosocial Competencies* (Rev. Ed.), by A. P. Goldstein, 1999, Champaign IL: Research Press.

The Prepare Curriculum: Stress Management Training

1. **Progressive Relaxation Training**
2. **Yogaform Stretching**
3. **Breathing Exercises**
4. **Physical Exercise**
5. **Somatic Focusing**
6. **Thematic Imagery**
7. **Meditation**

From *The Prepare Curriculum: Teaching Prosocial Competencies* (Rev. Ed.), by A. P. Goldstein, 1999, Champaign IL: Research Press.

The Prepare Curriculum: Cooperation Training

1. **Cooperative Learning**
   - **Student teams-achievement divisions**
   - **Teams-games-tournaments**
   - **Team assisted individualization**
   - **Jigsaw**
   - **Jigsaw II**
   - **Learning together**
   - **Group investigation**

2. **Cooperative Gaming**
   - **Ages 3-7:**
       Jack-in-the-box name game
       Cooperative hide-and-seek
       Partner gymnastics
       Frozen bean bags

   - **Ages 8-12:**
       New basketball
       Three-sided soccer
       Tug of peace
       All on one side

   - **Adolescent:**
       Strike-outless baseball
       Mutual storytelling
       Octopus massage
       Brussels sprouts

From *The Prepare Curriculum: Teaching Prosocial Competencies* (Rev. Ed.), by A. P. Goldstein, 1999, Champaign IL: Research Press.

Cooperative Gaming

1. Everyone who wishes to play can.

2. Everyone plays an equal amount of time via use of simultaneous games and frequent substitution when necessary.

3. Everyone has equal opportunity to play each position.

4. Players compete against own past performance, not each other.

5. Skill emphasis is on self-improvement.

6. No goals are counted, no points awarded, no score kept.

7. Extrinsic rewards (trophies, awards) are deemphasized.

8. Cooperative skills are actively encouraged, e.g., all must touch ball before a shot can be taken.

9. Multi-ball, multi-goal games are used.

10. Individual penalties are not announced to minimize reinforcement of attention.

11. Expulsion from game is used for deliberate attempts to injure another player.

The Prepare Curriculum: Understanding and Using Groups

1. **Forming**
   - The warm-up wave!
   - Breaking the ice
   - Graphics: self-disclosure activities
   - Being part of the group

2. **Storming**
   - Discrimination games
   - Trust-level disclosures
   - Model-building: an intergroup competition

3. **Norming**
   - Process observation: a guide
   - Role nominations: a feedback experience
   - Choosing new colors
   - The gift of happiness: experiencing positive feedback

4. **Performing**
   - Top problems: a consensus-seeking task
   - Stretching: identifying and taking risks
   - Line-up and power inversion: an experiment

5. **Adjourning**
   - Bus ride

From *The Prepare Curriculum: Teaching Prosocial Competencies* (Rev. Ed.), by A. P. Goldstein, 1999, Champaign IL: Research Press.

Successful Alternative Schools

- Remedial, not "soft jails"

- Clear and consistent academic and behavioral goals

- Motivated, empathic, and culturally diverse staff

- Responsiveness to individual learning styles

- Small class size

- High performance standards and expectations

- Daily attendance and progress reports

- Full days of study, rigorous workloads

- Continual monitoring and evaluation

- Mandatory student and parent counseling

- Administrative commitment and financial support

Aggression Reduction Strategies

Unproductive

- Punishment

- Catharsis

- Cohabitation

Productive

- Complexity

- Prescriptiveness

- Situationality

- Learned behavior

Delinquents on Delinquency: Punitive Strategies

- **Incarceration**

- **Harsher incarceration**

- **Mandatory incarceration**

- **Longer incarceration**

- **Sentence youths as adults**

- **Incarceration of parents**

- **Incarceration with attack dog**

- **Life sentences**

- **Life sentences without food**

- **Stricter parents and schools**

- **Involuntary drug rehabilitation**

- **Curfew**

- **More gun use by store owners**

- **House arrest by parents**

From *Delinquents on Delinquency*, by A. P. Goldstein, 1990, Champaign IL: Research Press.

Delinquents on Delinquency: Rehabilitative Strategies

- Early adoption of unwanted children
- School uniforms
- Longer school hours
- Learning how to think
- Classes on delinquency
- Self-esteem groups
- Pictures of the future
- Earlier work permits
- Counseling advertisements
- Closing of housing projects
- Videos of incarcerated youths
- Celebrity campaigns
- Less biased police
- Delinquents as store detectives
- Vans to pick up truants
- Alcohol-free bars and dances
- Psychologists at arcades
- Rewarding nondelinquency

From *Delinquents on Delinquency*, by A. P. Goldstein, 1990, Champaign IL: Research Press.

Punishment Moderator Variables

1. Likelihood of punishment

2. Consistency of punishment

3. Immediacy of punishment

4. Duration of punishment

5. Severity of punishment

6. Possibility of escape or avoidance of punishment

7. Availability of alternative routes to goal

8. Level of instigation to aggression

9. Level of reward for aggression

10. Characteristics of the prohibiting agents

School Suspension Categories

Insubordination

Fighting

Disruptive behavior

Vulgar and abusive language

Cutting class

Leaving the school building

Persistent disobedience

Loitering

Trespassing

Assaulting a student

Assaulting a staff member

Striking a student

Striking a staff member

Threatening a student

Threatening a staff member

Harassing a student

Harassing a staff member

Possessing an illegal drug

Using an illegal drug

Selling an illegal drug

Possessing drug paraphernalia

Possessing alcohol

Using alcohol

Reckless endangerment

Possessing/using a weapon/ dangerous object

Smoking

Theft

Arson

Extortion

Gambling

Destroying or defacing school/ personal property

Sexual harassment

Vandalism

Tardiness

Indecent exposure

Truancy

Failing to obey the reasonable request of a staff member

Leaving the classroom without permission

Being unprepared for class

Falsifying information

Possessing stolen property

Being in an area where an illegal drug/alcoholic beverage was being used

Possessing pornographic/obscene material

Being disrespectful/uncooperative

Refusing to stay for detention

Failing to follow in-school suspension rules

Multiple Causes of Aggressive Behavior

Causes	Examples
Physiological predisposition	Male gender, high arousal, temperament
Cultural context	Societal traditions and mores which encourage/ restrain aggression
Immediate interpersonal environment	Parental/peer criminology; aggressive models in movies and on TV
Immediate physical environment	Temperature, noise, crowding, traffic, pollution
Personal qualities	Self-control, repertoire of alternative prosocial values and behaviors
Disinhibitors	Alcohol, drugs, successful aggressive models
Presence of means	Guns, knives, other weapons
Victim characteristics	Gender; size; behavior during crime

Aggression Characteristics of Possible Prescriptive Relevance

- High Intensity vs Low Intensity
- Proactive vs Reactive
- Overcontrolled vs Undercontrolled
- Early Onset vs Late Onset
- Overt vs Covert vs Authority Conflict

Prescriptive Intervention by Type of Aggression

Proactive aggression	Reactive aggression
Object-oriented	Person-oriented
Goal: to obtain, dominate	Goal: to hurt, injure
Cold-blooded	Angry, volatile
Example: mugging	Example: aggravated assault
Crimes premeditated	Crimes of passion
Possible interventions:	Possible interventions:
Consistent punishment for aggression	Anger control training
Consistent reward for prosocial behavior	Empathy training
Social skills training	

Aggressive Incidents

- **Horseplay**
- **Rules violation**
- **Disruptiveness**
- **Refusal/defiance**
- **Cursing**
- **Bullying**
- **Sexual harassment**
- **Physical threats**
- **Vandalism**
- **Out-of-control behavior**
- **Student-student fights**
- **Attacks on teachers**
- **Use of weapons**
- **Collective violence**

From *Break It Up: A Teacher's Guide to Managing Student Aggression*, by A. P. Goldstein, J. Palumbo, S. Striepling, & A. M. Voutsinas, 1995, Champaign IL: Research Press.

Contextual Correlates and Causes of Aggression

There is more aggression:

In schools

> The larger the school
>
> In the cafeteria, stairwells, and bathrooms than in classrooms
>
> In March than in any other month
>
> In 7th grade than in any other grade
>
> With autocratic or laissez-faire school administrators than with "firm but fair"

In prisons

> The larger the prison
>
> The older the prison
>
> The more the external (in and out) traffic
>
> The more the internal (within) traffic
>
> The less the contact between the warden and prisoners
>
> The fewer the number of work assignments
>
> The less the education of the correctional officers

In sports

> By members of the home team than by the visiting team
>
> When the team is in the middle of its league standings
>
> Later in the game than earlier in the game
>
> Later in the season than earlier in the season
>
> Behind the net in hockey; near the 50-yard line in football

Corporal Punishment at Home

- **Legal in all 50 states**

- **Applied to 90% of U.S. children**
  - **56% slapped or spanked**
  - **31% pushed or shoved**
  - **10% hit with object**
  - **3% object thrown at child**

- **Peak application by age 3 to 4**

- **Still applied to 25% of U.S. adolescents**

- **Sons hit more than daughters**

- **Older parents less likely to hit**

- **Parents hit during adolescence are themselves more likely to hit**

- **Parents who hit each other are more likely to hit**

From *Beating the Devil Out of Them*, by M. A. Straus, 1991, New York: Lexington Books.

Corporal Punishment at School

- **Legal in 23 states**

- **Arkansas, Louisiana, Mississippi, Alabama highest**

- **700,000 instances per year in U.S.**

- **Disproportionately applied to**
    Minority youth
    Learning disabled youth
    Emotionally disturbed youth

- **School policy and procedure**
    Number of strokes
    Intensity of strokes
    Size of paddle
    Presence of a witness
    Prior parental approval

From *School Discipline and School Violence*, by I. A. Hyman, 1997, Boston: Allyn & Bacon.

Demonstrated Effects
of Television Violence

Aggression Effect

- Increased copycat violence
- Increased self-directed violence

Victim Effect

- Increased fearfulness
- Increased mistrust
- Increased self-protectiveness

Bystander Effect

- Increased desensitization
- Increased callousness

Copycat Violence

- **Males > females**

- **Younger > older**

- **Lower S.E.S. > middle or upper S.E.S.**

- **From program types:**
  Rank 1   Violently erotic
  Rank 2   Cartoon, sports, soap opera
  Rank 3   Adventure, detective, crime
  Rank 4   News, public affairs

- **Greater when the violence depicted is:**
  Justified
  Rewarded
  Involves a weapon
  Shown in specific "how-to" detail
  Shown frequently
  "Painless"

From "The Effects of Television Violence on Antisocial Behavior: A Meta-analysis," by G. A. Comstock & H. Paik, 1994, *Communication Research, 21,* pp. 516-546.

Television Violence:
What's a Parent to Do?

- Watch a few children's shows yourself; be your child.

- Plan viewing in advance; emphasize nonviolent shows.

- Monitor child's actual viewing; explain undesirability of initiating violence.

- Watch some shows with your child; contrast real and pretend.

- Provide interesting alternative activities, especially reading.

- Explain false or exaggerated commercial claims.

- Encourage legislation, television companies, and advertisers to increase nonviolent programming.

Aggression Replacement Training: Implementation of Productive Intervention Strategies

1. Complexity
Behavioral (Skillstreaming)
Affective (Anger Control Training)
Cognitive (Moral Reasoning Training)

2. Prescriptive
Lower social class learning style
Responsiveness to external authority (Modeling)

Action orientation (Behavioral rehearsal)

Focus on consequences (Performance feedback)

3. Situational/Contextual
Family intervention
Peer intervention
System intervention

4. Learned Behavior
Psychoeducational in both strategy and tactics

Part 6
Notes